20 Answers

೪

Jehovah's Witnesses

Trent Horn

Catholic
Answers
Press

20 Answers: Jehovah's Witnesses
Trent Horn
© 2015 Catholic Answers

Published by Catholic Answers, Inc.
2020 Gillespie Way
El Cajon, California 92020
1-888-291-8000 orders
619-387-0042 fax
catholic.com

Printed in the United States of America

978-1-941663-26-4
978-1-941663-27-1 Kindle
978-1-941663-28-8 ePub

Introduction

The doorbell rings, and you peer through the peep-hole. Standing on your doorstep is a man in a suit and a woman in a tasteful dress. They don't look like your average salespeople, so you open the door. It turns out they are here today to see if you "hope for a better world" or if you "wonder if the Bible is still relevant." They want you to have some free magazines and are willing to study the Bible with you at your convenience. It turns out that the guests on your doorstep are Jehovah's Witnesses, a religious group founded in the 1870s that has nearly 8 million members worldwide.

Jehovah's Witnesses differ from Catholics or Evangelical Christians because they reject certain fundamental Christian teachings. In one of its magazine articles, the group distinguishes itself from Protestantism:

> Protestant faiths reject certain features of Catholic worship, Reformation leaders retained certain Catholic dogmas, such as belief in the Trinity, hellfire, and the immortality of the human soul. Jehovah's Witnesses, however, believe that those doctrines not only contradict the Bible but also promote a distorted view of God.[1]

In place of these doctrines, Jehovah's Witnesses believe that Jesus is actually Michael the Archangel, that the wicked are annihilated instead of being sent to hell, and that only 144,000 people will go to heaven, while all other believers will live forever on a paradise Earth. Jehovah's Witnesses also differ from other denominations in that they reject as evil things most Christians consider to be harmless. For example, Jehovah Witnesses do not celebrate birthdays, secular holidays like Mother's Day, or even religious holidays like Christmas and Easter. They also do not take oaths of office, salute flags, or accept blood transfusions. For those who are considering becoming a Jehovah's Witness, it is crucially important to know what this group believes, and this booklet has been written to provide you with that information.

This booklet has also been written to give Catholics the tools they need to engage Jehovah's Witnesses in gracious dialogue. While this booklet is written for a Catholic audience, I have taken care to be respectful of Jehovah's Witnesses as individuals and to be accurate in my assessment of their beliefs. If you are a Jehovah's Witness, I encourage you to have an open mind to what I have written here.

I am not a former Jehovah's Witness, but I know that the Watchtower Bible and Tract Society (the official leadership of the Jehovah's Witnesses) has told you not to read literature that is critical of your religion. I know they distribute magazine articles that say things like, "What must we do to avoid false teachers? We do not speak to them or invite them into our houses. We also do not read their books, watch them on television, read what they write on the Internet."[2] But the Watchtower Bible and Tract Society also encourages non-Jehovah's Witnesses like me to give you a fair hearing and to not simply dismiss the Watchtower as being a "false prophet." If you expect other people to be willing to change their minds about Jehovah's Witnesses, then shouldn't you be willing to do the same?

1. What is the history of the Jehovah's Witnesses?

Jehovah's Witnesses emerged in the northeastern United States during the 1870s, though at the time they were known as "Bible Students." Under the direction of founder Charles Taze Russell, the Bible Students believed they had restored the true doctrines of the Christian faith that were lost after the death of the apostles. In 1881, Russell founded a printing company that was moved to Brooklyn, New York, where it became known as *The Watchtower Bible and Tract Society*. The corporation still exists there and serves as the legal and ecclesial authority for the Jehovah's Witnesses.[3] Russell used the press to spread the message that the world would come to an end in 1914.[4] When it didn't, Russell claimed that he had miscalculated and that the world would end in 1915.[5]

After Russell died in 1916, Joseph Franklin Rutherford succeeded him as the president of the

Watchtower Bible and Tract Society. In a book he published through the Watchtower called *Millions Now Living Will Never Die*, Rutherford claimed that many who were alive in 1914 would live to see the end of the world—which would now take place in 1925. Rutherford also predicted that the patriarchs Abraham, Isaac, and Jacob would be resurrected, and God would transform Earth into a paradise for the patriarchs as well as for the majority of believers.[6]

In order to accommodate the resurrected patriarchs, Rutherford had the Watchtower Society construct a mansion in San Diego, California, that was later called Beth Sarim, or "House of the Princes."[7] Even though the mansion was built four years after the failed 1925 prediction, Rutherford still preached the imminent end of the world and served as Beth Sarim's caretaker during the Great Depression.[8]

In 1931, Rutherford changed the group's name to *Jehovah's Witnesses* in order to distinguish it from other competing "Bible Student" sects, many of which still exist.[9] He also taught that God was the ultimate leader of the Jehovah's Witnesses, and the Watchtower Bible and Tract Society served as his official "administrator."[10] Rutherford died at Beth Sarim in 1942 and was succeeded by the Watchtower Society's third president, Nathan Knorr.

Knorr was instrumental in creating programs that trained Jehovah' Witnesses to deliver testimonies door-to-door. He also commissioned the publishing of a new translation of the Bible called the *New World Translation* (NWT). The NWT was published as a single volume in 1961, and the Watchtower claims this translation "offer[s] no paraphrase of the Scriptures. Our endeavor all through has been to give as literal a translation as possible."[11] However, several Greek scholars have criticized the NWT for translating certain passages in ways that sacrifice accuracy in order to promote Jehovah's Witness theology (see questions 8 and 14).

Beginning in the mid-1960s, the group's literature hinted strongly that the end of the world would come in 1975.[12] In 1969, the group's *Awake!* magazine said, "If you are a young person, you also need to face the fact that you will never grow old in this present system of things. Why not? Because all the evidence in fulfillment of Bible prophecy indicates that this corrupt system is due to end in a few years."[13] Despite this failed prediction, *Awake!* continued through the 1980s to print at the top of the magazine's first page the following text: "[T]his magazine builds confidence in the Creator's promise of a peaceful and secure world before the generation that saw the events of 1914 passes away."

The "events of 1914" refer to Jesus' invisible return, which the Watchtower claims was prophesied to happen 2,520 years after the fall of Jerusalem in 607 B.C., which would be A.D. 1914 (even though this contradicts mainstream historians, who agree Jerusalem fell in 587 B.C.).[14] Since there are only a handful of people alive today who were alive in 1914, it seems all but certain that this prophecy too will be invalidated. Perhaps that is why in 1995, after carrying the banner in the magazine for thirteen years, the reference to the generation of 1914 was replaced with dateless prediction of a world "that is about to replace the present wicked, lawless system of things."

In response these failed predictions, Jehovah's Witnesses claim that the Watchtower is not infallible and admit on their official website, "[W]e have had some wrong expectations about the end. But we are more concerned with obeying Jesus and saving lives than with avoiding criticism."[15] While it is noble to be ready for Jesus' return, these failed predictions call into question the truth of the Watchtower's claim to be "Jehovah's channel of communication"[16] (see question 19).

Despite these setbacks, membership in the group has climbed steadily over the years, and today there are approximately 8 million Jehovah's Witnesses worldwide.[17] What's remarkable about this growth is that Jehovah's Witnesses have an incredibly high turnover rate. According to one *Time* magazine article, "[T]wo-thirds of the people who told [the surveyors] they were raised Jehovah's Witnesses no longer are— yet the group attracts roughly the same number of converts."[18] The article attributes this steady growth to the group's zeal for door-to-door evangelism.

2. What is the religious life of a Jehovah's Witness like?

In order to distinguish themselves from what they consider "apostate Christendom,"[19] Jehovah's Witnesses do not call their place of worship a "church." Instead, on weekends (usually a Sunday) Jehovah's Witnesses meet for about an hour and a half in a building called a Kingdom Hall.[20] The hall serves as the central meeting place for a particular "mission territory," and weekend meetings are open to the public. The congregants dress in formal clothes (shirt and tie for men, dresses for women) and greet one another as "brother" or "sister." They are usually welcoming to newcomers and make it a point to tell them that no monetary collection is ever taken.

Each meeting opens and closes with a brief prayer, while the majority of the time is spent listening to a presentation related to the Bible or studying an article published in one of the Watchtower's magazines. Instead of pastors or priests, experienced congregants called "elders" oversee the meetings, because Jehovah's Witnesses do not believe there should be any distinct "clergy" class.

After the weekend meetings, most Witnesses go through their assigned neighborhood and evangelize on people's doorsteps. They might also host a table stocked with Jehovah's Witness literature in a public area like an airport or city park. In any case, they carry booklets with titles like "What Does the Bible Really Teach?", as well as the group's official magazines like *The Watchtower* or *Awake!* If a person is receptive to the Witnesses' message, his home is scheduled for a return visit. If the person continues to have an interest in the group, he is invited to a Bible study where it is hoped he will make the decision to join the organization. In order to convert, he must demonstrate a thorough knowledge of Jehovah's Witnesses doctrine by answering more than a hundred questions before a local elder.[21] If the person demonstrates sufficient knowledge, as well as the right intentions, he is baptized by full immersion after answering "yes" to the following questions:[22]

1. "On the basis of the sacrifice of Jesus Christ, have you repented of your sins and dedicated yourself to Jehovah to do his will?"

2. "Do you understand that your dedication and baptism identify you as one of Jehovah's Witnesses in association with God's spirit-directed organization?"

The new convert is expected to do as much missionary work as possible in order to spread the good news about Jehovah. Young people are encouraged to choose university majors that are useful in "pursuing a theocratic career," while the retired are discouraged from "taking it easy" and are urged instead to use their new free time to continue in ministry work.[23] Some Witnesses called "pioneers" devote themselves to more than seventy hours of witnessing each month.

The intense focus on evangelism includes the requirement for all adult members to submit monthly "field reports" that detail how many hours they've spent "in the field" and how many converts they've received through baptism. In 2013, Jehovah's Witnesses spent a combined 1.8 *billion* man-hours evangelizing, though they celebrated only 277,344 baptisms. This means that, on average, a Witness must evangelize in the field eight hours a day, every day of the week, *for two years* before seeing one convert.[24]

A Witness who fails over a sixth-month period to submit a field report is deemed an "inactive publisher." According to the Jehovah's Witnesses' website, "Those who were baptized as Jehovah's Witnesses but no longer preach to others, perhaps even drifting away from association with fellow believers, are *not* shunned. In fact, we reach out to them and try to rekindle their spiritual interest. . . . If, however, a baptized Witness makes a practice of breaking the Bible's moral code and does not repent, he or she will be shunned or dis fellowshipped."[25]

This means that the person's friends and family may not speak to him, or even acknowledge his existence, unless he publicly repents (although communication among family living in the same home is still accept-able). A Witness can be disfellowshipped if he is found guilty of engaging in immoral behavior or of "aposta-sy," which includes openly renouncing membership in the organization. This makes it difficult for doubting members to leave the group, because it will cost them their relationships with their friends and family.

3. Are Jehovah's Witnesses Christians?

The central belief of Jehovah's Witnesses is that there is one God and his name is Jehovah. According to the Jehovah's Witnesses, Jehovah created a "Son" and it was through this Son that he created the rest of the world. This Son has the same "spirit nature" as his Father, which makes him "a God" or "a mighty God." How-ever, the Son is still a creation of the Father, and so he is not the "true God" or he is not the "almighty God." Jehovah's Witnesses say those titles belong only to Jeho-vah, not Jesus. As a result Jehovah's witnesses pray only to Jehovah and never to the Son. An article in *Awake!* magazine says, "[T]rue Christians do well to direct their worship only to Jehovah God, the Almighty."[26]

In contrast, Catholics (along with Protestants and Eastern Orthodox Christians) believe, as the Nicene Creed states, that Jesus is "God from God, light from light, true God from true God, begotten not made, one in being with the Father. Through him all things were made." The God of Christianity is one being who exists as three persons: the Father, Son, and Holy Spirit.

Since a Christian is someone who worships the God of Christianity, a person cannot be a Christian unless he worships the one God who has revealed himself as three co-equal and co-eternal divine persons. If a person faithfully follows what the Jehovah's Witnesses teach, then he would not be a Christian since he would deny essential truths about the Christian faith such as the divinity of Christ. Jehovah's Witness would probably say in response to this that they reject the decisions of manmade councils like Nicaea as well those councils' definitions of Christianity. They insist that the Bible affirms what they believe, and Catholics, Protestants, and Eastern Orthodox are the real heretics.

For example, some Witnesses say the Bible teaches there is one *almighty* God, but there are also many lesser gods, one of which is Jesus. They might quote Psalm 86:8 which says, "There is none like thee among the gods, O Lord"; and Psalm 82:1 says, "God has taken his place in the divine council; in the midst of the gods he holds judgment." In John 10:31–34, Jesus confronts the Jewish leaders who accuse of him of blasphemy for "making himself God." Jesus answers them by quoting the psalms: "Is it not written in your law, 'I said, you are gods'?"

But in the Bible, human rulers and judges are sometimes called "gods," such as in Exodus 22:9, which uses the Hebrew word for God, *Elohim*, to refer to human judges. Jesus quoted Psalm 82 because it criticizes human judges like the Pharisees who were wicked and fell short of the moral standard set by God. Psalm 82:7 says those "elohims" will "die like men," so these beings were not actual gods. Jesus' point in John 10:31–34 is that if the corrupt human leaders in Psalm 82 could be called "gods," then why can't Jesus, whom "the Father has sanctified and sent into the world" (John 10:36), be called God? After all, Jesus actually *is* God! Indeed, John 5:18 says the Jewish leaders wanted to kill Jesus because he was "making himself equal with God."

Jehovah's Witnesses also cite the part of 1 Corinthians 8:6 which says, "[Y]et for us there is one God, the Father, from whom are all things and for whom we exist," as proof that only the Father is God. But this interpretation ignores the rest of the verse, which says, ". . . and one Lord, Jesus Christ, through whom are all things and through whom we exist." If Jesus can be our "one Lord," even though the Bible also says the Father is Lord (Mark 13:20, Luke 4:18, Acts 17:24), then the Father can be our "one God" even though, as we will see, there are many Scripture verses that say Jesus is God.

4. How do Jehovah's Witnesses respond to the testimony of John's Gospel that Jesus is God?[27]

In order to avoid the force of John 1:1 and John 8:58, the Jehovah's Witnesses' New World Translation

(NWT) of the Bible renders these verses differently than almost every other translation of the Bible. For example, the last part of John 1:1 is translated in the NWT, "The Word was *a* God," instead of just "The Word was God," which makes Jesus a "lesser God" and not the "almighty God." Jehovah's Witnesses are taught early in their Bible studies to say something like this in response to John 1:1: "The correct translation is 'The Word was a god' not 'The Word was God,' because the Greek word for 'God' in this passage, or *theos*, does not have the article [the word *the*] in front of it."

But the NWT is inconsistent in its own translation principles. For example, it translates John 1:5, "There came a man who was sent as a representative of God; his name was John." Here also, the Greek word *theos* lacks an article, but the verse is not translated, "There came a man who was sent as a representative of *a* God; his name was John."

If John 1:1 had put the article before God (so that it read in its original Greek *ho logos en ho theos*), it would be translated "the Word was the God," which would imply that "the Word" and "the God" are the same entity. This would plunge us headlong into the heresy of *modalism*, or the belief that God and Jesus—or more precisely, the Father and Jesus—are the same person. Christians believe that the Father and the Son are two separate persons while still being the same God, because God is not one *person*. God is instead one *being* who exists as a Trinity of three persons. Indeed, Matthew 28:19 says that we are baptized in the *name*—not the *names*—of the Father, Son, and Holy Spirit, which implies these three persons are one being.

Regarding John 8:58, most Bibles translate the passage, "Before Abraham was, I AM." The NWT, on the other hand, translates the passage, "Before Abraham came into existence, I have been." According to the Watchtower, Jesus was merely claiming *preexistence*, or being a very old part of Jehovah's creation.[28] He was not claiming to be Jehovah himself, since he did not utter the sacred divine name "I AM."

Is there a good reason to think John 8:58 should be translated, "Before Abraham was, I have been" instead of "Before Abraham was, I am?" In Greek, the verse reads, "prin Abraam genesthai ego eimi." The part we are concerned with is the last part, *ego eimi*. *Ego* means "I," and *eimi* is the Greek word for the verb "to be." When John 10:9 reads "ego eimi he thyra," we translate it as Jesus saying, "I am the door," not "I have been the door." *Ego eimi* is a simple phrase to translate in Greek, and it makes sense to translate "ego eimi" in John 8:58 as "I AM," not "I have been."

Finally, when it comes to Thomas' exclamation to Jesus, "My Lord and my God" (John 20:28), some Jehovah's Witnesses say that Thomas was so overcome with joy that he didn't know what he was saying. But in other Scripture passages we are told explicitly when the apostles say something they don't mean. After Jesus' transfiguration, Peter says impulsively that he will build tents for Jesus, Moses, and Elijah. In response to this exclamation, Luke notes that Peter did "not know what he said" (Luke 9:33), while Mark says of Peter, "He did not know what to say, for they were terrified" (Mark 9:6). Secondly, Jehovah's Witnesses can't say Thomas was not speaking to Jesus, because in their official New World Translation of the Bible, John 20:28 says, "In answer Thomas said to him: 'My Lord and my God!'" So, Thomas didn't merely say, "My Lord and My God!" He said it *to* Jesus.

Whenever an apostle or angel is mistaken for God in the New Testament, the worshipped person corrects those who are worshipping him. When the Greeks in Lystra mistook Paul and Barnabas for the gods Zeus and Hermes, the two men tore their garments. They reminded the crowd that they were humans and implored them to worship the true God who made heaven and earth (Acts 14:14–15). In Revelation 19:10, the apostle John falls at the feet of an angel to worship him, but the angel tells him, "You must not do that!" Yet Jesus did not correct Thomas. This should lead us to the conclusion that, when it came to Thomas's statement of faith, there was nothing to be corrected. If that is the case, then we should imitate Thomas and not be afraid to address Jesus as our "Lord and God" as well.

5. How do Jehovah's Witnesses respond to other Scripture verses that support the deity of Christ?

In Isaiah 43:11, God says, "I am the LORD, and besides me there is no savior." But in Titus 2:13, St. Paul tells Christians we are "awaiting our blessed hope, the appearing of the glory of our great God and Savior Jesus Christ." Not only does this passage say that Jesus is our savior (a title that belongs to God alone), it says Jesus is our God. To get around this passage, the NWT renders Titus 2:13 "while we wait for the happy hope and glorious manifestation of the great God and of our Savior, Jesus Christ," which implies that only the title "savior" belongs to Jesus and not "Great God." Jehovah's Witnesses then say that the Bible sometimes describes human beings as saviors, such as Othniel in Judges 3:9, and so its description of Jesus as our savior does not mean Jesus is God.

While it is true that humans can be saviors in a limited sense, only God can save us from sin, and it is this kind of salvation that is attributed to Jesus. Furthermore, we have good reason to believe that both "God" and "savior" in Titus 2:13 apply to Jesus because of a rule in Greek grammar called Granville Sharp's rule. Basically, this rule applies in the following circumstances:

1. You have two nouns that are not proper names like Jesus or Paul.

2. The first noun has an article in front of it but the second does not.

3. Both nouns are connected by the word *and* (in Greek *kai*).

In 2 Peter 1:11 we see the rule applied in the following passage: "So there will be richly provided for you an entrance into the eternal kingdom of our Lord and Savior Jesus Christ." In this case, "Lord" and "Savior" are not proper names; the Greek word translated "Lord" has an article, but the Greek word translated as "Savior" does not, and both words are connected by the word *and*. We can conclude from Sharp's rule that both "Lord" and "Savior" refer to the same person, Jesus Christ (the NWT renders 2 Peter 2:11 in this way also). Since Titus 2:13 has an almost identical sentence structure to 2 Peter 1:11, why not translate it the same way and say that Jesus is both savior and "great God?"

Another passage where Jesus is called God is Colossians 2:9. In this passage, Paul says of Christ, "For in him the whole fullness of *deity* [emphasis added] dwells bodily." However, the NWT renders this verse, "For in him the fullness of *the divine quality* dwells bodily [emphasis added]." To say Jesus has the fullness of "divine quality" instead of "deity" could mean Jesus is like God but not fully God. But Paul doesn't use the Greek word that means "divine quality" (or *theiotes*) in this passage.

He instead uses the Greek word *theotes,* which means that the very essence of the thing in question is God.[29]

Finally, there are other verses of Scripture that describe people treating Jesus in a way that only God should be treated. For example, the book of Acts records how the first martyr, Stephen, said, "Lord Jesus, receive my spirit" before he was stoned to death (Acts 7:59. Some Jehovah's Witnesses say Stephen wasn't praying to Jesus but merely speaking to him, since he saw Jesus in a vision. The problem with this explanation is that Stephen's vision is described in Acts 7:55. By verse 59 the Sanhedrin has already taken Stephen to another location, which means that the vision probably did not continue, and therefore Stephen was simply praying to Jesus. Finally, if Stephen's belief was in line with that of Jehovah's Witnesses, why didn't he say, "Lord, receive my spirit" or "Jehovah God, receive my spirit"? Since Stephen could licitly pray to Jesus at death, then Christians should be able to pray to Jesus instead of Jehovah, because Jesus is Jehovah, the true God (see question 15).

6. What Scripture verses do Jehovah's Witnesses use to prove that Jesus is not God?

One Watchtower magazine article states, "Jesus, the Son of God, never claimed to be equal to or of the same substance as his Father. Rather, he said: 'I am going my way to the Father, because the Father is greater than I am' (John 14:28). He also told one of his followers: 'I am ascending to my Father and your Father and to my God and your God' (John 20:17)."[30]

First, let's look at John 14:28 in its full context. After Jesus reassures the apostles that he will send them the Holy Spirit to teach them all things, he says in John 14:27–28, "Peace I leave with you; my peace I give to you; not as the world gives do I give to you. Let not your hearts be troubled, neither let them be afraid. You heard me say to you, 'I go away, and I will come to you.' If you loved me, you would have rejoiced, because I go to the Father; for the Father is greater than I."

Why would the apostles rejoice because Jesus is going to someone who is a "greater God" than he? How would Jesus' return to a being that is greater than he comfort the disciples, who don't want to see Jesus leave them? What makes more sense is that when Jesus says the Father is "greater," he means the Father holds a higher *position* than he. Christ was in a "lesser" position than the Father during his earthly ministry, because he set aside his divine glory in order to become a man (Philippians 2:7).

During his earthly life, Jesus was "a little lower than the angels" (Heb. 2:7), but, after his Resurrection, Jesus was given "the name which is above all other names" (Phil. 2:9). The fact that Jesus is returning to his original status alongside the Father in order to sit at his "right hand" (Acts 7:55) means he has an equal position with the Father, which is indeed cause for rejoicing. The disciples should not mourn Jesus leaving, because Jesus is going to reign as their "Lord and God" (John 20:28).

But what about John 20:17? According to the critic, Jesus can't be God because Jesus calls another person God. Therefore, it must be *that* person, or the Father, who is God and not Jesus. But if God is more than one person, then the Son can both acknowledge his Father as God and still be God himself. One has to assume that God can't be more than one person in order for this objection to work.

But why would Jesus talk about another God if he himself is God? Remember, after the incarnation Jesus possessed both a fully divine nature and a fully *human* nature. Part of what it means to be human is to acknowledge God and to worship him, so, as a man, Jesus would give worship to the Father and recognize that he is God.

However, notice that even in his exchange with Mary Magdalene Jesus makes a distinction between "my Father" and "your Father" and "my God" and "your God." Jesus never says "our God" or "our Father." This implies that God is a Father to Mary Magdalene and the apostles in a different sense than he is a Father to Jesus. Specifically, they (and us) have God as an *adoptive* father (Romans 8:15), while Jesus is the one and only begotten Son of God (John 1:18). We are *like* God, because God gives us his grace as adopted children; but Jesus *is* God, because he shares the same nature as the Father.

A Jehovah's Witness might also ask, "Why doesn't the Bible call Jesus 'God' as opposed to the Son of God?" Along with pointing to scripture passages like John 1:1 and Titus 2:13 that do call Jesus God, you could also ask him how many true Gods there are. The Witness will say, "One," and then you may ask, "If the son of a dog is a dog, and the son of a human is a human, then what is the Son of the true God?" If he says, "A God," but not "the true God," ask him, "So, if Jesus is not the true God, is he a false god?"

Hebrews 1:3 says that Jesus "bears the very stamp of his nature, upholding the universe by his word of power." Who else but the true God fits this description? Remember, only by assuming the true God is one *person* is a Jehovah's Witness able to claim that it is impossible for both Jesus and the Father to be the one true God. He must be ready to defend this assumption if he challenges the doctrine of the deity of Christ, so a good question to ask is, "Where in Scripture does the Bible teach that God is only one person?"

7. Why do Jehovah's Witnesses believe that Jesus is one of God's creations and is not the "almighty God" or the Creator himself?

One Watchtower article says of Christ, "He is 'the beginning of the creation by God.' (Rev. 3:14). As 'the firstborn of all creation,' [Colossians 1:17] he lived for aeons in heaven with his Father, Jehovah."[31] Does calling Jesus "the beginning" or "the first-born" of creation imply that Jesus was the first created thing?

In Revelation 3:14, the Greek word translated "beginning" is *arche*, which can also mean *ruler, source,* or *origin*.[32] Indeed, in Revelation 21:6 the Father calls himself "the beginning," but this does not mean the Father had a literal beginning. What makes more sense is that Jesus is the *source* of all creation since other parts of Scripture (John 1:3, Colossians 1:15–17) teach that Jesus created "all things."

In regards to Colossians 1:15–17, the Greek word for "firstborn," *prototokos,* can refer to a special position someone has that is worthy of honor and privilege and not only to a literal order in childbirth among siblings. For example, in Psalm 89:27 God says of David, "I will make him the first-born, the highest of the kings of the earth." Obviously, David was not the first king to reign among the kings of the Earth. He was instead placed in a position of preeminence or authority over all other kings. But just as the firstborn of kings is the one who rules over kings, it follows that the firstborn of creation is the one who rules over creation.

In addition, we know Christ cannot be a created thing, because Paul makes it clear that in Christ "*all things* were created, in heaven and on earth, visible and invisible, whether thrones or dominions or principalities or authorities—*all things* were created through

26

him and for him. He is before *all things*, and in him *all things* hold together" (emphasis added).

How could Jesus create *all things* if he were part of creation itself? Did Jesus create himself, too? Jehovah's Witnesses recognize this problem, and that's why their Bible mistranslates Colossians 1:16–17 by adding the word "other" to the passage. In the NWT the passage reads, "because by means of him all *other* things were created in the heavens and on the earth. . . . All *other* things have been created through him and for him. Also, he is before all *other* things, and by means of him all *other* things were made to exist" (emphasis added).

One Watchtower article says, "Jesus is the sole *direct* creation of God. The only-begotten Son is the one through whom God created all other things—Colossians 1:16."[33] But no Greek word that can be translated as "other," such as *heteros* and *allos*, is in the original Greek text of Colossians 1:16–17. Jehovah's Witnesses insist that the word "other" is implied in the text, because Colossians 1:15 says Christ is "the firstborn of creation," which means Jesus is a part of the creation by being its firstborn, or eldest part.

But while the word *of* can mean "part of a larger whole" it can also mean "having supremacy over."[34] Since verses 16–17 say Jesus created *all things*, and this is unambiguous in the text, they help us understand what verse 15 means. Therefore, it makes more sense to consider verse 15 as referring to Christ having authority over creation instead of being the first part of creation.

Finally, when discussing the issue of creation with Jehovah's Witnesses, it's helpful to point to a passage like Isaiah 44:24, where God said, ""I am the LORD, who made all things, who stretched out the heavens alone, who spread out the earth—Who was with me?" According to the Witnesses, Jehovah created the physical universe through Jesus (Colossians 1:15–17); but this contradicts Isaiah 44:24, which says God *alone* created the physical world. The only way to resolve this contradiction and show that God alone created the universe is to accept that the Jesus is God along with the Father, so only one God created the universe, even if God is more than one person.

8. Is it true that Jehovah's Witnesses believe that Jesus is actually Michael the Archangel?

Jehovah's Witnesses believe that, before he became a man, Jesus was Michael the Archangel, and ever since his Ascension into heaven he is Michael again. Jehovah's Witnesses believe this because, first, they already believe Jesus is the highest or most glorious of God's creatures. Since they consider archangels to be the highest of the angels, Jehovah's Witnesses believe Jesus must be one. Second, according to Jehovah's Witnesses, "The Bible describes Michael as *the archangel,* implying that he alone bears that designation. Hence, it is reasonable to conclude that Jehovah God has delegated to one, and only one, of his heavenly creatures full authority over all other angels."[35] If Jesus is an archangel, and Michael is the only archangel, it follows that Jesus and Michael must be the same person.

The Witnesses also claim, "The only other verse in which an archangel is mentioned is at 1 Thessalonians 4:16, where Paul describes the resurrected Jesus, saying: 'The Lord [Jesus] himself will descend from heaven with a commanding call, with an archangel's voice and with God's trumpet.' So Jesus Christ himself is here identified as the archangel, or chief angel."[36]

This argument is not persuasive for several reasons. First, calling Michael *the* archangel in Jude 1:9 no more proves that Michael is the only archangel anymore than calling Felix *the* Cat proves he is the only cat.[37] 1 Thessalonians 4:6 even uses the phrase "*an* archangel's" voice and not "*the* archangel's voice," implying that there is more than one archangel. Second, just because Jesus is described as descending with an archangel's voice it doesn't mean he is an archangel. The same verse says Jesus will descend with God's trumpet, but that doesn't mean Jesus is a trumpet. It only means Jesus' voice will be of the quality of an archangel's voice or that he will be accompanied by angels who will shout for him. Finally, this argument works only if we already believe Jesus is the highest of the angels and is not God.

But the Bible teaches that Jesus is not an angel. Hebrews 1:4–6 says Jesus has "become as much *superior to angels* as the name he has obtained is more excellent than theirs. For to what angel did God ever say, 'Thou art my Son, today I have begotten thee'? Or again, 'I will be to him a father, and he shall be to me a son'? And again, when he brings the first-born into the world, he says, '*Let all God's angels worship him*'" (emphasis added).

Angels don't worship other angels; they worship only God. Since Jehovah's Witnesses believe Jesus is Michael the archangel, the NWT avoids the situation of angels worshipping another angel by rendering this passage, "And let all of God's angels do obeisance to him." *Obeisance* means to bow down in respect for another person. In Exodus 18:7, Moses made obeisance to his father-in-law, Jethro; and in 1 Kings 1:16, Bathsheba bowed before King David. These instances of obeisance merely describe paying solemn respect to someone. They do not describe the kind of worship one would give to God.

The Greek word in Hebrews 1:6 that Jehovah's Witnesses translate "obeisance" is *proskuneo*. This word can refer to simple bowing or a showing a sign of respect to someone in authority. But it can also refer to the kind of worship given to God alone. The NWT renders *proskuneo* as "worship" when the verb has

God the Father as its direct object, and even when the word is used to describe the worship of a false god, such as the Beast in Revelation 13. But when *proskuneo* is used of Jesus, the NWT always translates it as "obeisance" and never as "worship."

While this may be appropriate in some verses that only describe paying respect to Jesus, there are other verses where the word *worship* seems to be the most appropriate word to use, such as Luke 24:52 and Matthew 28:9, which refer to the apostles worshipping Jesus after his Resurrection; or Matthew 14:32, where the apostles worship Jesus after he calms the storm and say, "Truly you are the Son of God." The Jehovah's Witnesses absolute use of *obeisance* in reference to Jesus is most likely driven by their theology and not by a careful study of the texts describing worship of Jesus as a divine person.

9. What are some other objections Jehovah's Witnesses make to the deity of Christ?

Most of the objections Jehovah's Witnesses make to the deity of Christ involve one of the following three errors:

- They assume that to be greater in position means being greater in being.

- They assume that God is only one person.

- They assume that Jesus has only one (divine) nature.

Let's start with objections based on the first assumption. The Watchtower says, "First Corinthians 11:3 states: 'The head of the Christ is God.' In fact, the Son will always be in subjection to God. (1 Corinthians 15:28) The Scriptures therefore show that Jesus is not God Almighty. Instead, he is God's Son."[38] But 1 Corinthians 11:3 also says the head of every woman is man, but does this mean that men are greater in being or "ontologically superior" to women? No! Just as women are equal to men while having a role that involves service, Christ is equal to God while having a role that involves service. As John 14:28 showed us, because the Father may be greater than Jesus in position or function, it doesn't follow that Jesus is a lesser *being* than the Father.

Other common objections to the deity of Christ work only if one assumes beforehand that God can only be a unitary person. Jehovah's Witnesses might say that, if Jesus is God, then who was Jesus praying to in the Garden of Gethsemane—himself? The answer is that Jesus was praying to the Father, and the Father is God. But this does not mean Jesus is not God, because God is not one person. Jesus would be praying to himself only if Christians taught that Jesus is the *Father*, not if they taught that Jesus is God.[39] Instead, we teach that Jesus is God and the Father is God. But God was not "praying to himself" because, once again, *God is more than one person.* God is one being who exists as three persons (Father, Son, Holy Spirit), each of whom has an eternal relationship with the other two persons of the Trinity.

Finally, many objections to the deity of Christ misunderstand the doctrine and take it to mean that Jesus has one (divine) nature, a fact which seems to be contradicted by Jesus' human existence. These critics say, "God can't die, but Jesus died on the cross so therefore Jesus can't be God. But the Church teaches that everything Jesus did God the Son did because Jesus and God the Son are the same divine person.[40] Jesus is a divine person who, in addition to his divine nature, took on a human nature through the incarnation. This allowed Jesus to engage in "human" acts without ceasing to be God.

For example, when Jesus' human soul left his human body, Jesus (and consequently God the Son) died on the cross. Of course, God the Son did not cease to exist, because Jesus' soul is immortal and fully conscious, even apart from his body. This allowed Jesus to take up his life again as he predicted he would in John 2:19.[41]

The fact that Jesus is fully man and fully God also explains another Scripture verse that Jehovah's Witnesses say proves Jesus is not God. 1 Timothy 2:5 says, "For there is one God, and there is one mediator between God and men, the man Christ Jesus." The Witnesses say that in order for Christ to be a mediator between humanity and God he can't be God because concept of a mediator *between* God and man wouldn't make sense if God were the mediator. But if that argument is true, then how could Jesus be man, since the humbler party *seeking* mediation can't itself be the mediator? Jesus is able to mediate between God and man because Jesus is both fully human and fully divine. This allows Jesus to cross the "infinite gap" between God and man to redeem all mankind.

10. How do Jehovah's Witnesses respond to the testimony of the early Church Fathers who said Jesus was God?

In their booklet "Should you believe in the Trinity?", the Jehovah Witnesses claim that the early Church Fathers did not believe that Jesus was God. Even though the booklet is now out of print, Jehovah's Witnesses occasionally cites these quotations in order to promote the mistaken view that early Christians denied what are now considered essential doctrines of the Christian faith. Let's examine three of the Church Fathers they most commonly cite:[42]

Justin Martyr (died A.D. 165): The Watchtower says, "Justin calls the prehuman Jesus a created angel who is "other than the God who made all things."—He said that Jesus was inferior to God and "never did anything except what the Creator . . . willed him to do and say."

Here is what Justin actually says in his dialogue with the rabbi Trypho: "I shall attempt to persuade you, since you have understood the Scriptures, [of the truth] of what I say, that there is, and that there is said to be, another God and Lord subject to the Maker of all things; who is also called an Angel, because He announces to men whatsoever the Maker of all things—above whom there is no other God—wishes to announce to them."[43]

First, as we will see with the other Fathers, Justin did not have the same trinitarian vocabulary that later Christians possessed, so we can expect his theological formulations to be imprecise. But there is still within those formulations a core set of beliefs that is incompatible with what the Watchtower teaches. For example, notice that Justin calls Jesus "God," even though earlier in the dialogue Justin says, "There will be no other God, O Trypho, nor was there from eternity any other existing, but He who made and disposed all this universe."

Justin acknowledges that Jesus is God but without saying there are two Gods (one being "almighty" and the other being just "mighty"). Justin says Christ is an angel only because he functions like an angel in announcing good news. In fact, the word Greek word *angelos* can be translated either "angel" or "messenger." Finally, just because Jesus only does the Father's will does not mean he isn't God. It's means only that he is the obedient son of God who himself is "God."

Clement of Alexandria (died A.D. 215): The Watchtower says, "Clement of Alexandria called Jesus in his pre-human existence 'a creature' but called God 'the uncreated and imperishable and only true God.' He said that the Son 'is next to the only omnipotent Father' but not equal to him."

The phrase "but not equal to him" is a comment by the anonymous author of this Watchtower pamphlet; it is not in Clement's original writings. In fact, Clement says just the opposite in his work *Exhortation to the Heathen*: "He that is truly most manifest Deity, *He that is made equal to the Lord of the universe*; because He was His Son, and the Word was in God"[44] (emphasis added).

Tertullian: The Watchtower quotes Tertullian saying, "There was a time when the Son was not. . . . Before all things, God was alone.'"

What Tertullian means in this passage is that even though the person we now call "the Son" is eternal, he did not always have the title of "Son" but became that when the Father sent him to create the world. Of course, Catholics now recognize this as a heresy, but we can acknowledge that Tertullian was correct when he said that the Son is God and not merely "a god." He writes, "That there are two gods and two Lords, however, is a statement which we will never allow to issue from our mouth; not as if the Father and the Son were not God, nor the Spirit God, and each of them God; but formerly two were spoken of as gods and two as

Lords, so that when Christ would come, *he might both be acknowledged as God and be called Lord*, because he is the Son of him who is both God and Lord"[45] (emphasis added).

The other passage that speaks of God being alone leaves out a critical qualification Tertullian makes: "Moreover, He was alone, because there was nothing external to Him but Himself. Yet even not then was He alone; for He had with Him that which He possessed in Himself, that is to say, His own Reason."[46] Tertullian goes on to explain that this reason is the *logos*, which is the same word John uses in his Gospel to describe Christ before his incarnation. According to Tertullian, God was alone with the Word, but, as John says in his Gospel, "The Word was God."

While the writings of the Fathers are not inspired and contain some errors (such as Tertullian's denial of the preexistence of the Son), they provide a valuable window into early Christian beliefs and show that the early Church was Catholic in its theology. It bears hardly any resemblance to what the Watchtower teaches.

11. What do Jehovah's Witnesses believe about the Holy Spirit?

Jehovah's Witnesses not only deny that the Holy Spirit is God, they deny that the Holy Spirit is a person. Instead, they consider the Holy Spirit to be God's "active force" that he uses to affect the world. Because of this belief, they do not capitalize the name Holy Spirit and sometimes they do not even include the pronoun "the." For example, in the New World Translation, John the Baptist says that Jesus "will baptize you with holy spirit and with fire" (Luke 3:16).

One common argument against the Holy Spirit being a person is that the spirit fills or anoints people. One Watchtower magazine article says, "The holy spirit is not a person. Early Christians 'became *filled* with holy spirit,' and Jehovah said: 'I shall *pour out* some of my spirit upon every sort of flesh.' (Acts 2:1–4, 17)."[47] The Jehovah's Witnesses' popular evangelism handbook *Reasoning from the Scriptures* says of the Holy Spirit that people "can be 'baptized' with it; and they can be 'anointed' with it. (Luke 1:41; Matt. 3:11; Acts 10:38) None of these expressions would be appropriate if the holy spirit were a person."[48]

It's true an embodied being cannot fill another embodied being without killing it, but the Holy Spirit is not embodied or made of matter. There is no reason that an immaterial person cannot be present inside a material human being. After all, in John 14:23, Jesus says that both he and the Father can dwell inside a man's heart. The fact that the Father and Son can do this does not prove they are inanimate forces but rather that they are the unlimited God who is omnipresent, everywhere at all times.

Furthermore if the Holy Spirit is just God's active force, then how can it lead us into all truth or be our advocate as Jesus says *he* (not "it") is in John 14:26? The Witnesses try to explain this away by saying that, "While some texts say that the spirit 'spoke,' other passages make clear that this was done through angels or humans . . . none of the expressions found in these texts in themselves prove that the holy spirit is a person."[49] But is this actually true?

Acts 13:2 describes how the Spirit spoke to a group of teachers and prophets in Antioch. It says, "While they were worshipping the Lord and fasting, the Holy Spirit said, 'Set apart for me Barnabas and Saul for the work to which I have called them.'" Acts 10:19–20 says, "And while Peter was pondering the vision, the Spirit said to him, 'Behold, three men are looking for you. Rise and go down, and accompany them without hesitation; for I have sent them.'" There's no mention of any other humans or angels through whom this inanimate spirit is speaking. Indeed, Paul says in Romans 8:27, "And he who searches the hearts of men knows what is the mind of the Spirit, because the Spirit intercedes for the saints according to the will of God." If someone has a mind and intercedes for us, what else are we supposed to think of this being except that he is a person?

But the Holy Spirit isn't just any person. The Holy Spirit will guide us into all truth (John 16:13), and he alone comprehends the thoughts of God (1 Corinthians 2:11). Who else but God can know all truth or comprehend God's thoughts? In fact, St. Peter shows us the Holy Spirit is God when he asks Ananias, who lied and held back money due to the apostles, "Ananias, why has Satan filled your heart to lie to the Holy Spirit and to keep back part of the proceeds of the land? . . . How is it that you have contrived this deed in your heart? You have not lied to men but to God" (Acts 5:3–4). Not only is the Holy Spirit a person who can be lied to, but lying to the Holy Spirit is the same as lying to God himself, because the Holy Spirit is the third person of the Holy Trinity.

12. What do Jehovah's Witnesses believe about the Trinity?

Jehovah's Witnesses say the Trinity is "the lie that made God a mystery"[50] and is simply "not a Bible teaching."[51] In order to refute these accusations, it's important to have a correct understanding of what the Trinity actually is. Put simply, the doctrine of the Trinity teaches that God is one *being* who exists as three co-eternal and co-equal *persons*: Father, Son, and Holy Spirit. Just as there are beings that are zero persons (like rocks) or beings that are one person (humans and angels) God is one being who is three persons. Each divine person is not a "part" of God but is fully God, because each person of the Trinity fully possesses a divine nature.

Many objections to the Trinity can be answered by explaining what it actually is. For example, when Jesus was tempted to worship the devil, he famously refused and responded by quoting the Old Testament's command to "worship the Lord your God, and him only shall you serve" (Luke 4:8). The Watchtower says of this passage, "Jesus made it clear that there is just one God who must be worshipped when he said 'him alone,' not 'us,' which he *would* have said if he were part of a Trinity."[52] But the Trinity *does* teach that there is just one God to be worshipped, and this God is a unity that can be referred to as "him." God is not a collection to be referred to as "us" but three persons united in *one* being, each of whom fully possess the divine nature.

Most Jehovah's Witnesses criticisms of the Trinity focus on trying to disprove the divinity of Christ and the divinity of the Holy Spirit. They recognize that if either of these two persons is referred to as God (not just *a* god, but the almighty God), then the Trinity logically follows, because Jehovah's Witnesses are already committed to the idea that there is only one "almighty God." Reviewing the answers to questions 3–11 will be helpful in defending the Trinity in this respect.

Other Jehovah's Witnesses criticisms of the Trinity try to prove that the doctrine is unintelligible or is a pagan belief that was assimilated into Christian doctrine and is not biblical. For example, one Watchtower article says, "The Trinity, explain Catholic scholars Karl Rahner and Herbert Vorgrimler, 'could not be known without revelation, and even after revelation cannot become wholly intelligible.' Can you really love someone who is impossible to know or understand? The doctrine of the Trinity, therefore, is a barrier to knowing and loving God."[53]

But this objection confuses being *incomprehensible* with being *unintelligible*. Yes, the Trinity cannot be fully *comprehended*, or understood in every respect. But just because something is not "completely intelligible" it does not follow that it is unintelligible, or nonsense. Jehovah's Witnesses even admit that their God Jehovah is not completely understandable. *Reasoning from the Scriptures* says, "Should we really expect to understand everything about a Person who is so great that he could bring into existence the universe, with all its intricate design and stupendous size?[54]

Since there is nothing else in the universe like the Trinity, we can expect that there are things we don't understand about this doctrine, even though on the whole the doctrine is not a logical contradiction. The Trinity is a mystery, but that does not mean it is some unknowable "black hole." Rather, a theological mystery refers to truths that we would not know if God had not revealed them to us. It is, like other mysteries of the faith, "not taught by human wisdom but taught by the Spirit" (1 Cor. 2:13).

The Watchtower also claims the term *Trinity* is a pagan one derived from ancient mythology and is not found in the Bible. Now, it is true that the word itself does not appear in Scripture, but neither do the words *Governing Body, generation of 1914, kingdom hall*, or other words associated with many important Witnesses doctrines. This shows that a doctrine does not have to appear in the Bible in order for it to be true. Furthermore, the claim that the Trinity is based on mythological "triads" of gods such as Osiris, Isis, and Horus in Egypt is false. These pagan triads are nothing like the Trinity, because they represent three different and competing gods, while the Trinity is one God who is three co-equal, co-eternal persons or as Tertullian wrote in A.D. 216, "The unity is distributed in a Trinity. Placed in order, the three are the Father, Son, and Spirit."[55]

13. Why do Jehovah's Witnesses think that God's name is Jehovah?

In the Old Testament, God's name is spelled with the consonants YHWH. It is derived from Exodus 3:14, when God says his name is "I am who I am," which in Hebrew is *Ehyeh Asher Ehyeh*. The four letters representing God's name, what is called the sacred tetragrammaton, was eventually considered so holy that the Jewish people did not speak it. This was done to ensure that no one broke the second commandment, "You shall not take the Lord's name in vain." But this presented a problem, because when the Jewish people read the Old Testament, they encountered the name YHWH more than 6,000 times. In order to read the text, they replaced YHWH with the Hebrew word for Lord, or *adonai*.

Over time, this practice caused the original pronunciation of the name to be lost, but Jewish sources have not accepted the pronunciation "Jehovah."[56] The rendering of "Jehovah" came about in the eleventh century, when monks combined the Latin rendering of the tetragrammaton, or JHVH, with the vowels in the word *Adonai*, which gave us *Jah-hov-ai*, or Jehovah. But why is it so important to know that God's name is Jehovah? According to the Watchtower, "It is important not only to know but also to use that name. Why? Because the Bible tells us: "Everyone who calls on the name of Jehovah will be saved."—Romans 10:13; Joel 2:32."[57]

But Romans 10:13 doesn't say everyone who calls on the name of *Jehovah* will be saved. It says, "Everyone who calls on the name of the *LORD* will be saved," or, in Greek, "Everyone who calls on the name of the *Kurio* will be saved." The name Jehovah, or any variation of that name, is not found in any New Testament manuscripts. This brings us to one of the oddest features of the New World Translation of the Bible. Whenever the word "Lord" (or *kurios*) is found in the New Testament, the NWT renders it "Jehovah"—with a few curious exceptions. Look how the NWT renders Romans 10:

> For if you publicly declare with your mouth that Jesus is *Lord*, and exercise faith in your heart that God raised him up from the dead, you will be saved. For with the heart one exercises faith for righteousness, but with the mouth one makes public declaration for salvation. For the scripture says: "No one who rests his faith on him will be disappointed." For there is no distinction between Jew and Greek. There is the same Lord over all, who is rich toward all those calling on him. For everyone who calls on the name of *Jehovah* will be saved (emphasis added).

If the NWT were consistent, it would render Romans 10:9, "For if you publicly declare with your mouth that Jesus is *Jehovah* and exercise faith in your heart that God raised him up from the dead you will be saved."

If calling on the name of Jehovah is so important to our salvation, then why does the New Testament tell us to call upon another name instead? Acts 4:10–12 says, "[B]y the name of Jesus Christ of Nazareth . . . there is salvation in no one else, for *there is no other name under heaven given among men by which we must be*

45

saved." In Philippians 2:9–11, Paul says, "Therefore God has highly exalted him and bestowed on him *the name which is above every name*, that at the name of Jesus every knee should bow, in heaven and on earth and under the earth, and every tongue confess that *Jesus Christ is Lord*, to the glory of God the Father" (emphases added).

If using the name Jehovah was so important, then why is it not cited anywhere in the New Testament? Why doesn't Jesus say to pray to Jehovah when he teaches his disciples to say the Lord's Prayer? Some Witnesses claim that the name "Jehovah" did appear in the original New Testament manuscripts, but later heretical scribes removed it. However, there is no evidence from any ancient manuscripts for this claim, and so it is just an unprovable, and dismissible, conspiracy theory.

14. What do Jehovah's Witnesses believe about Christ's Passion?

Jehovah's Witnesses believe that the Greek word translated as "cross" in the New Testament, or *stauros*, actually means "upright stake," or in their words, a "torture stake." They claim that Jesus was nailed through both wrists on a large vertical stake without a crossbeam. They even go so far as to claim that, "true Christians do not use the cross in worship."[58]

Oddly enough, this belief was not present in the earliest doctrines of the Jehovah's Witnesses. Their second president Joseph Rutherford taught that, "The cross of Christ is the greatest pivotal truth of the divine arrangement, from which radiate the hopes of men."[59] It was not until the late 1930s that Rutherford changed the Witness's position on this issue.

However, if a "stake" were used instead of a cross, then why does John 20:25 refers to the *nails* that were used to affix Jesus to the cross. This means that Jesus' arms were stretched out on a cross and one nail was driven through *each* arm, not one nail through both arms on a stake. In addition, Matthew 27:37 says, "over his head they put the charge against him, which read, 'This is Jesus the King of the Jews.'" But if Jesus were crucified on a stake, then the sign would be placed directly above his hands, not his head.

We also have evidence that shows the early Christians believed Jesus was crucified on a cross, not a stake. The 2nd century apologist Justin Martyr eloquently described the cross beams used to crucify Jesus.[60] In the 3rd century Tertullian said that Christians used the Greek letter *tau,* or a T, as a sign of the cross.[61] Biblical scholar Larry Hurtado has even shown how Christian writers in the second century combined the Greek letters for T and R in order to create a symbol that represented the crucifixion called a *staurogram* that looks like a person on a cross.[62]

Finally, an ancient drawing called the Alexamanos graffito shows a roman soldier worshipping a man with a donkey head being crucified. It has been dated to the early third century and was intended to mock Christians who worshipped a crucified God. The caption reads, "Alexamanos worships [his] God." Tertullian even references such parodies in his own writings.[63]

Another unique Jehovah's Witness belief about Jesus' Passion is the belief that Jesus was not raised physically from the dead but rather that his spirit was raised. Jehovah's Witnesses usually cite 1 Peter 3:18 and 1 Corinthians 15:45, 50 in defense of this belief, stating that Jesus was "put to death in the flesh, but made alive in the spirit" and "[Jesus] became a life-giving spirit . . . [for] flesh and blood cannot inherit the kingdom."

But as New Testament scholar N.T. Wright says, "The 'flesh/spirit' antithesis of 3:18 and 4:6 sounds to modern western ears as though it stands for our 'physical/non-physical' distinction; but this would take us down the wrong path."[64] These verses simply mean that Jesus no longer has a corruptible and mortal body like ours (or "flesh and blood body"). Instead Jesus has a body infused with supernatural power, or spirit, that makes it "incorruptible" without being immaterial.

Finally, the Witnesses' theory that Jesus rose from the dead only spiritually contradicts Jesus' prophecy that he would raise up "the temple of his body" three days after his death (John 2:19). It also contradicts

Luke 24:39, where the risen Jesus says to the disciples, "See my hands and my feet, that it is I myself; handle me, and see; for a spirit has not flesh and bones as you see that I have."

15. What do Jehovah's Witnesses believe about death and hell?

Jehovah's Witnesses believe that the immortality of the human soul is a myth derived from Greek philosophy and is not taught in the Bible. Jehovah's Witnesses instead teach that "[w]e cease to exist when we die, but this does not mean that everything is necessarily finished."[65] Most Watchtower publications soften the reality of this teaching by teaching the doctrine of "soul-sleep." One article says, "[T]he dead are unconscious; they are in a condition best compared to sleep. Thus, we need not worry about what happens to us after death, any more than we worry when we see someone sleeping soundly."[66]

Of course, when we see someone sleeping, we don't worry, because they still exist! However, the Jehovah's Witnesses teach that upon death we "cease to exist" and that we are resurrected (or to be more accurate, a copy of ourselves is created) at the final judgment. To support this belief, the Watchtower cites several Old Testament verses that seem to support the idea that death is the end of a human being's existence:

"The soul that sinneth, it shall die."
—Ezekiel 18:4, King James Version

"For the living know that they will die, but the dead know nothing, . . . for there is no work or thought or knowledge or wisdom in Sheol, to which you are going."
—Ecclesiastes 9:5, 10, Revised Standard Version

First, we know by reason alone that the soul can't be destroyed, because it isn't composed of any material parts. A thing can be destroyed only when its parts are disassembled, and since the soul has no distinct parts, it can't be destroyed.[67] Secondly, the language in these passages is not always meant in a literal sense. Ecclesiastes is merely using phenomenological language to describe how the dead appear to *us* while Ezekiel is using the word "soul" to refer to a whole human being, not just his immaterial part (like how we might say there are "100 souls on that sinking ship").

Relying on a few passages in the Old Testament to teach about the nature of the soul is dangerous because some Old Testament writers had a dim view of the afterlife. For example, Job 7:9 and even Ecclesiastes 9:6 seem to deny that there could be *any* resurrection from the dead, something that Jehovah's Witnesses would not agree with. That's why we need to look at scripture in its entire context to see what it teaches on the nature of the soul.

For example, Jesus spoke to Moses at the transfiguration even though Deuteronomy 34:5 clearly says Moses died in Moab. John saw the deceased martyrs in heaven praising the Lord (Revelation 6:9–11) and Peter says that Jesus "preached to the spirits in prison" after he was crucified. But these descriptions of the afterlife would be impossible if human beings cease to exist at death. Paul even spoke of his own death and his desire "to depart and be with Christ, for that is far better" (Phil. 1:23). If Paul were unconscious after death, then how could that be better than life?

The Watchtower also claims, "When nominal Christians adopted the myth of the immortal soul, this led them to accept another myth—the teaching of hellfire."[68] Jehovah's Witnesses reject the teaching that any human being will spend eternity in hell, But in doing that they reject Jesus' own words in Matthew 25:46 where he says the wicked, "will go away into eternal punishment, but the righteous into eternal life."

The NWT mistranslates what Jesus says and renders the words "eternal punishment" into "everlasting cutting-off." in order to support the Witnesses belief that the wicked do not go to Hell but are instead destroyed or annihilated. They say this is justified because the Greek word rendered "punishment" in this passage, or *kolasin*, is derived from a word that means to "prune" or "cut off." Therefore, Hell is just separation from God by being annihilated or destroyed and not eternal, conscious punishment.[69] But analyzing a word's meaning from its etymology can lead to gross errors.

After all, the word *virtue* is derived from the Latin word *vir* which means "man," but that doesn't mean all virtuous people are "manly" people. As any Greek dictionary will tell you, *kolasin* simply means "punishment." Also, how can someone be forever cut off from something if they are annihilated and cease to exist? We don't talk about a painting that catches fire being eternally destroyed, or being everlastingly cut off from an art museum. It's destroyed, period. Likewise, Jesus is making a comparison between the eternal life that the righteous will forever enjoy and the eternal punishment the wicked will forever endure. The comparison doesn't make sense if the wicked are simply destroyed.

16. What do Jehovah's Witnesses believe about heaven?

While most Christians believe their citizenship is in heaven (Philippians 3:20), Jehovah's Witnesses believe that the vast majority of believers will not go to heaven. Instead, they will live on a renewed "paradise earth," while 144,000 anointed Christians will rule over them alongside Jesus in heaven.[70] The Watchtower originally taught that, prior to 1935, all faithful Jehovah's Witnesses were part of the heavenly class of 144,000 who would go to heaven.

Those born before 1935 who believed they were part of the heavenly anointed class would partake of the bread and wine that was offered once a year at the Witnesses' memorial of the Lord's death. Each year, out of millions of Witnesses who attend, only a few thousand partake in the bread and wine offered at the service. However, in 2007 this teaching was changed. Prior to 2007, the Watchtower taught that anyone who identified as part of the anointed class who was well under 90 years old was thought to have been selected to replace one of the original 144,000 anointed before 1935 who later sinned or apostatized but that no new Christians were going to heaven."[71]

But in a 2007 article, the Watchtower said, "[T]he number of genuine anointed ones who have become unfaithful is likely not large . . . as time has gone by, some Christians baptized after 1935 have had witness borne to them that they have the heavenly hope. (Romans 8:16, 17) Thus, it appears that we cannot set a specific date for when the calling of Christians to the heavenly hope ends."[72] This means that an untold number of Christians have been, and still may be, called to go to Heaven and 1935 is no longer a special "cut-off year." It's fortunate for the Witnesses that this doctrine was changed, because in 2007 only two out of fifteen members of the Governing Body, which should comprise only anointed Christians, were born before 1935 (both of whom died in 2010).

Is there any biblical support for these teachings? The Jehovah's Witnesses' claim that only 144,000 Christians will be in heaven comes from their interpretation of Revelation 7 and 14. But a closer look at those passages indicates that the 144,000 are all celibate Jews from the twelve tribes of Israel. Why does the Watchtower believe this aspect of Revelation is symbolic but that the *number* of people in heaven is literal? In the Bible, the number 1,000 usually symbolizes a large amount of things. Since 144,000 is 144 x 1,000, it makes sense to say that the number is a symbolic representation of the large number of Christians from all different parts of the Earth who will be present in heaven.

What about the Witness's practice of excluding from the Eucharist all but a select few? This contradicts Jesus' teaching in Scripture that partaking in the Eucharist is what causes someone to be able to go to heaven (John 6:53–57), not a sign that they are going to heaven. The Bible and the Church Fathers make no mention of only an anointed class of Christians being allowed to partake of the Eucharist. Instead, as early as the second century, Church Fathers like Justin Martyr said that anyone who held the Catholic Faith and was baptized could receive "the flesh and the blood of that incarnated Jesus."[73] Jesus also never divided believers into those who have an "earthly" hope and a "heavenly" hope. The Bible speaks only of those who are written in the Book of Life and will gain access to heaven and those who names are not in the book and will be damned for all eternity (Revelation 3:5, 20:15).

The Bible does speak of a new heaven and new earth, but the two will be one reality, not separated domains, that will replace the current heaven and earth, which will "pass away" (Rev. 21:1). Jehovah's Witnesses also support their view by quoting passages such as Matthew 5:5, where Jesus says the meek will inherit the Earth. But in Matthew 5:8, Jesus says the pure in heart will "see God," and in verse 10 he says the persecuted will receive the kingdom of heaven. Jesus is not saying these different people will receive different gifts but that holy people who follow God will receive abundant spiritual blessings in general.

17. What are some other distinctive Jehovah's Witnesses beliefs?

Along with their denial of traditional Christian doctrines like the Trinity, the divinity of Christ, the immortality of the soul, and the existence of hell, Jehovah's Witnesses are also distinctive for their rejection of the following practices.

Celebrating birthdays and holidays
Jehovah's Witnesses do not celebrate birthdays, because they claim such celebrations are pagan in origin,

and the Bible never records believers celebrating them. Instead, the only birthday parties that are recorded in the Bible are of evil men such as Pharaoh (Genesis 40:20) and King Herod (Mark 6:21), who executed people during these celebrations. But the Bible never describes the *celebrations* as being wicked or evil. Instead, it was the *men* being celebrated who were guilty of wrongdoing.

As to the objection that birthdays are a pagan practice Christians should not emulate, the Church teaches that the good or neutral things in non-Christian culture can be "baptized" and used for Christian purposes.[74] The Pantheon in Rome was once a pagan temple, but now its architectural beauty is used to glorify the only true God. This reasoning also applies to the Jehovah's Witnesses practice of not celebrating holidays due to their allegedly pagan origins.

Serving in the military

Jehovah's Witnesses do not serve in any nation's armed forces, do not hold political office, do not vote, and do not salute any nation's flag, even if refusal to do these things results in imprisonment or death. But nowhere in Scripture are Christians forbidden to serve in the military. In Acts 10, the centurion Cornelius converted to the Christian Faith but was not asked to stop serving in the military. When a group of soldiers asked John the Baptist what they must do to attain the kingdom, John simply told them to not extort anyone for money (Luke 3:14). John never said the soldiers could not lawfully earn money by being soldiers. Of course, we must never obey a civil law that causes us to violate God's commands (Acts 5:29), but we are also called to defend the helpless and protect them from evildoers, which for some may include military service.

Receiving blood transfusions

Jehovah's Witnesses believe that the Old and New Testaments' prohibitions on eating blood (Leviticus 17:10–15, Acts 15:20, 29) mean that it is a grave sin to receive blood via a medical transfusion. Witnesses carry medical cards that tell doctors they refuse any blood transfusions. The Witnesses' magazine *Awake!* even dedicated an issue to children who died from not receiving blood transfusions. They described these children as "youths who put God first."[75]

However, Witnesses are allowed to receive "blood fractions," the individual components of blood such as hemoglobin or albumin. But this is like saying a person who is not allowed to drink soda is allowed to drink corn syrup and eat sugar provided he doesn't combine the ingredients. Hopefully the Watchtower will end its prohibition on blood transfusions just as it ended its previous prohibition against vaccines in 1952.[76] Perhaps the Watchtower will allow Witnesses to follow their conscience on this issue just as it allows them to decide for themselves if contraception is moral (even though, unlike blood transfusions, the Bible does record an act of contraception that displeased God in Genesis 38:9–10).[77]

In regards to biblical arguments made against blood transfusions, Orthodox Jews still uphold the laws in Leviticus, including those related to blood. They methodically bleed animals before cooking them so as not to ingest any blood, but even they do not consider blood transfusions to be a sin. They understand that the spirit of the Old Testament law was to honor the life of an animal and discourage pagan rituals. It was not mean to forbid all uses of blood.[78]

Furthermore, if one were following all the prohibitions in Leviticus, he'd have to never eat animal fat, because Leviticus 3:16–17 says, "All fat is the LORD's. It shall be a perpetual statute throughout your generations, in all your dwelling places, that you eat neither fat nor blood." Likewise, the New Testament's prohibitions about blood refer only to engaging in a dietary practice that was scandalous to Jewish converts, not to something intrinsically immoral, because "[Jesus] declared all foods clean" (Mark 7:19). As such, the Church has the authority to dispense with this rule as being no longer necessary.

Ultimately, the issue of what these verses, as well as what the rest of the Bible, teaches about God, Christ, and salvation can be settled only by asking, "Who has the rightful authority to interpret Scripture and declare what it teaches?" A Jehovah's Witness can reject these arguments from Scripture as the products of "apostate Christendom" only as long as he relies on the Watchtower's official interpretation of these verses. In order to effectively engage a Witness in dialogue, we must critically examine the Watchtower's claims of having divine authority.

18. What do Jehovah's Witnesses believe about the great apostasy?

The central claims of the Watchtower, that it is God's "organization on earth" can only be true if God's true Church, or the Catholic Church founded on the apostles, perished from the face of the earth. But what if that never happened? If God's church did survive the death of the last apostle, then the Jehovah's Witnesses' claims to being God's true organization (which God, for some inexplicable reason, waited 1800 years to restore) is completely baseless. So is there any evidence that this supposed "Great Apostasy," or destruction of God's original Church, ever took place?

Some Witnesses cite Scripture verses that describe those who fell away from the Faith in the early Church, such as 2 Thessalonians 2:3, 2 Timothy 1:15, and Galatians 1:6–7. These verses show only that *some* members of the Church fell away from the Faith, not all of them.

This happens in all religions, including the Jehovah's Witnesses. After the death of Charles Taze Russell, many of his followers went on to start "Bible movements" that exist to this very day and do not recognize the authority of the Watchtower, but Jehovah's Witnesses would not take that as evidence that God's "organization" perished from the Earth. What the Jehovah's Witnesses need to show is that there was a *total* or *universal* falling away from the Faith in the first century, but the evidence does not support this conclusion.

For example, in 2 Timothy 1:15, Paul laments how the Christians in Asia Minor turned away from *him*, not Christ. Paul is saddened that these Christians did not come to his aid when he was placed under arrest. He is not speaking of a total apostasy. In 2 Thessalonians 2:2–3, Paul is speaking of events that will take place at the Second Coming of Christ. There will be people then who will rebel against God, but in 1 Thessalonians 4:17 Paul says there will still be faithful Christians who will be caught up to the Lord.

Along with the lack of evidence that a total apostasy took place, there is positive evidence that such an apostasy could never have taken place. Acts 1:20 describes how the apostles could pass on their authority to future bishops; and in Matthew 16:18–19, Jesus says to Peter, "I tell you, you are Peter, and on this rock I will build my church, and the powers of death shall not prevail against it. I will give you the keys of the kingdom of heaven, and whatever you bind on earth shall be bound in heaven, and whatever you loose on earth shall be loosed in heaven."[79] The Watchtower vigorously denies that the authority of the apostles was passed on after their deaths or that Peter ever had such authority to pass on.

It writes, "Augustine argued that it was Jesus on whom the church, that is the Christian congregation, was built, not Peter."[80] Augustine actually said he was not sure whether the "rock" in Matthew 16:18 referred to Peter, Jesus, or something else. He said, "Which of these interpretations is more likely to be correct, let the reader choose." But Augustine was adamant that what keeps him in the Catholic Church is "the succession of priests . . . beginning from the very seat of the Apostle Peter, to whom the Lord, after His resurrection, gave it in charge to feed His sheep, down to the present episcopate."[81]

In Matthew 28:20, Jesus says, "I am with you *always* until the end of the age"; and Paul writes in Ephesians 3:20–21, "To him be glory in the church and in Christ Jesus to all generations, for ever and ever. Amen." How would Jesus make sure the Church would endure for all generations?

Church Father Clement of Rome reminds his readers that Jesus foresaw there would be trials for the Church and took steps to keep these trials from destroying the Church. He writes in A.D. 96, "Our apostles knew through our Lord Jesus Christ that there would be strife for the office of bishop. For this reason, therefore, having received perfect foreknowledge, they appointed those who have already been mentioned and afterwards added the further provision that, if they should die, other approved men should succeed to their ministry."[82]

19. Are there any good reasons to believe the Watchtower Bible and Tract Society is "God's visible organization" on Earth?

In 1931, the Watchtower said that its magazine "is not the instrument of any man or set of men, nor is it published according to the whims of men. No man's opinion is expressed in The Watchtower. God feeds his own people, and surely God uses those who love and serve him according to his own will."[83] Jehovah's Witnesses believe that a group of people called "the faithful and discrete slave," which is an image from Jesus' parable in Matthew 24:44–47, is tasked with the job of "spiritually feeding" God's people.

In its early years, Jehovah's Witnesses believed that Charles Taze Russell was the slave. In 1927, Joseph Rutherford taught that the faithful and discrete slave was the special class of 144,000 anointed Christians who would go to heaven. As late as 2005 the Watchtower distinguished the Governing Body in Brooklyn from the larger "slave class." It said, "Christ thus leads the congregation by means of the spirit-anointed 'faithful and discreet slave' and its Governing Body."[84]

In 2012, the Watchtower chose to no longer distinguish the groups: "That slave is the small, composite group of anointed brothers serving at world headquarters during Christ's presence who are directly involved in preparing and dispensing spiritual food. When this group work [sic] together as the Governing Body, they [sic] act as 'the faithful and discreet slave.'"[85]

The Watchtower makes it clear that one's salvation depends on trusting and obeying the faithful and discrete slave. One Watchtower article says, "Without the assistance of 'the faithful and discreet slave,' we would neither understand the full import of what we read in God's Word nor know how to apply it."[86] And in another place, "Since Jehovah God and Jesus Christ completely trust the faithful and discreet slave, should we not do the same?"[87] Finally, one article goes so far as to say, "Just as Noah and his God-fearing family were preserved in the ark, survival of individuals today depends on their faith and their loyal association with the earthly part of Jehovah's universal organization."[88]

Anyone thinking of joining the Jehovah's Witnesses should ask himself, "Do I believe that God actually created this organization? What evidence is there for this extraordinary claim?"

Jehovah's Witnesses do not appeal to any miraculous intervention from God as proof that the Watchtower has his authority. Sometimes the Jehovah's Witnesses say the Watchtower is God's organization because it fulfills biblical prophecy. However, the examples they give to support this claim are vague and could apply to anyone. One article lists eighty Bible verses and says the faithful and discrete slave class can be identified as "Noah's wife," "the man in linen," "the locusts" in Revelation 9:3, and, finally, simply as "Jehovah's Witnesses."[89]

Others will say that the Watchtower is God's organization because it is the only group that possesses the correct interpretation of Scripture and the only group to have restored the true doctrines of the Faith. But this argument assumes what it tries to prove, that the Watchtower is God's authority and therefore it possess the correct interpretation of Christian doctrine and revelation.

In fact, many Watchtower publications that speak of the faithful and discrete slave who possesses Christ's authority don't present any arguments or evidence for this claim. In the 2005 book *Organized to Do Jehovah's Will*, the Watchtower says, "There are many reasons to have complete trust in the slave class. First and foremost, Jesus has appointed them over all his precious 'belongings.' This is a clear indication that he has complete trust in them."[90]

But notice that this is simply an assumption dressed up as evidence. In other words, "How do you know Jesus has given the Watchtower special authority? Because Jesus *did* indeed give the Watchtower special authority!"

Organized goes on to say, "Second, God's Word admonishes Christians to cooperate fully with those taking the lead. . . . Through much hardship and experience, the slave class has demonstrated that the spirit of God is with it."[91] Once again, these reasons to could apply to any church, including the Catholic Church, which has a better claim to having served God for nearly 2,000 years "through much hardship and experience."

Jehovah's Witnesses claim that the apostles represented the first-century "governing body," and now the modern governing body operates with the same authority. Notably absent from such a claim is an explanation of why Church fathers like Clement claimed to receive that authority from the apostles themselves or an explanation of how an organization founded 1,800 years after the deaths of the apostles actually has this authority.

Along with the paucity of evidence for the Watchtower's claim to authority, there is also the fact that the leaders of the Watchtower Bible and Tract Society have routinely failed to predict the end of the world, marking off the years 1914, 1915, 1925, and 1975 (among others) as being the date of Armageddon.

But Deuteronomy 18:22 states that a person is not a prophet if he makes a prediction that fails to come to pass (or if he leads the people away to worship false gods). Jehovah's Witnesses will claim that the organization is not acting as a prophet and false predictions are signs that God is giving the Watchtower " new light" or new understanding of doctrine.[92] But not only does this contradict previous Watchtower claims to being "God's prophet,"[93] it also leads to an intractable problem: if the Watchtower is "still learning," why trust anything it teaches now? If God were really guiding the Watchtower, then why would he allow his "spirit-led" organization to lead so many people into error about the end of the world? The simplest answer to these questions is that the Watchtower should not be trusted because it is guided by men, not God.

20. How should I share my faith when I encounter Jehovah's Witnesses?

Even though this booklet has provided several scriptural replies to the Watchtower's doctrines, engaging in biblical debates with the Witnesses isn't usually the best course of action. The Witnesses are skilled at wielding dozens of memorized verses to defend their beliefs. Even if you skillfully reply to these verses with a sound biblical argument of your own, the Witnesses can always dismiss your argument by saying that's just your (incorrect) interpretation.

Jehovah's Witnesses are told that all other Christian churches have been founded by Satan and that only the Watchtower Bible and Tract Society serves as God's "faithful and discrete slave." In order to make headway with the Witnesses, you must challenge this foundational belief.

Stay focused on one issue: authority

Ask the Witnesses to explain why you should believe 1) that the Catholic Church lost its God-given authority and the apostles were unable to pass it on to their successors and 2) that the Watchtower is God's official organization on Earth whose teachings and decisions represent his will. Instead of saying, "Jehovah's Witnesses believe X" or "You people believe X," always phrase your objections in the form of, "Why does the Watchtower teach X?" or "I have a hard time accepting that God leads the Watchtower in light of X." This will make the Witnesses less defensive and less inclined to feel you are attacking them personally.

Only when the Witnesses begin to see that the Watchtower is untrustworthy can they be open to seeing which Church really does have God's authority. You can then ask them why they believe in the Bible and show them that the Catholic Church best explains why we can trust the canon of Scripture we have today (since the Watchtower came into existence more than a millennia after the canon of the Bible was set).

Do make it personal

Jehovah's Witnesses spend countless hours studying and practicing for conversations with potential converts.

Most of these dialogues focus on answering arguments about the Bible, but hardly any prepare the Witnesses for personal discussions. It's important for you to get the missionaries "off script" and focused on their own personal lives and their relationship with God. If they mention that they are former Catholics, this can be a good opportunity to discuss any mistaken views of the Church they may hold.

Do take into account their attitude toward "apostates"
If you offer the Jehovah's Witnesses this booklet or any other literature, they will either refuse it or they will take it and discard it. The Watchtower warns its followers that literature critical of Jehovah's Witnesses doctrine is dangerous, and it is a grave sin for them to read it. The Watchtower compare such literature to pornography or an infectious disease that is to be avoided at all costs.[94] Be sure to call out the Witnesses' double standard of being unwilling to read opposing literature while expecting *you* to read *their* literature.

Don't be rude
This should go without saying, but use only language that you would be comfortable with others using in reference to you. Therefore, you shouldn't refer to the guests at your front door as being members of a cult that has brainwashed them. How would you respond to a Protestant who said that the Catholic Church was

a cult? You would probably be unreceptive to his message, no matter what he had to say.

Instead, you should always be mindful to follow the example of 1 Peter 3:15: "Always be prepared to make a defense to any one who calls you to account for the hope that is in you, yet do it with gentleness and reverence."

About the Author

Trent Horn is an apologist and speaker for Catholic Answers. He specializes in pro-life issues as well as outreach to atheists and agnostics. He holds a master's degree in theology from Franciscan University of Steubenville.

Endnotes

1   "Are Jehovah's Witnesses a Protestant Religion?" *The Watchtower*, November 1, 2009, 19. http://wol.jw.org/en/wol/d/r1/lp-e/2009813.

2   "Will You Pay Attention to Jehovah's Clear Warnings?" *The Watchtower* (Simplified), July 15, 2011, 11–12. http://wol.jw.org/en/wol/d/r1/lp-e/402011524.

3   In 1955 the group's name was slightly amended and is now the Watchtower Bible and Tract Society *of Pennsylvania*.

4   *Zion's Watch Tower*, July, 15 1894, 226.

5   Charles Taze Russell, "The Time Is At Hand" *Studies In the Scriptures Series II*, page 1915, 99, 101, 242.

6   Joseph Rutherford, *Millions Now Living Will Never Die* (Brooklyn: International Bible Students Association, 1920), 89–90.

7   Joseph Rutherford. *Salvation* (Brooklyn: Watchtower Bible and Tract Society, 1939), 311.

8   "Judge Awaits Next Coming of King David" *Syracuse Herald Journal*, March 23, 1930, page 4.

9   These include the Dawn Bible Students and the Free Bible Students among many other groups.

10 "Religion vs. Theocracy" *Consolation* 21 no. 547, September 4, 1940, 25.

11 "How Can You Choose a Good Bible Translation?" *The Watchtower*, May 1, 2008, 22.

12 *The Watchtower*, May 1, 1970, 273.

13 *Awake!*, May, 22 1969, 15.

14 See Carl Olof Jonsson's 2004 book *The Gentile Times Reconsidered* for a thorough critique of the Witnesses' claim that Jerusalem was

destroyed in B.C. 607.

15 "Should You Fear the End of the World?" *The Watchtower*, January 1, 2013, 8. http://www.jw.org/en/publications/magazines/wp20130101/should-you-fear-end-of-world/.

16 "The Bible-A Book Meant to Be Understood," *The Watchtower*, October 1, 1994, 8.

17 *2014 Yearbook of Jehovah's Witnesses*. (Brooklyn: Watchtower Bible and Tract Society, 2013) 176.

18 David Van Biema, "America's Unfaithful Faithful" *Time Magazine*, February 25, 2008.

19 "Rome's Many Faces" *Awake!*, July 8, 2001, 15–16.

20 "What is a Kingdom Hall?" *The Watchtower*, May 1, 2010, 31. http://wol.jw.org/en/wol/d/r1/lp-e/2010331.

21 *What does the Bible really teach?* (Brooklyn: Watchtower Bible and Tract Society, 2005) 182. The questions asked by the elders can be found in *Organized to do Jehovah's will* (Brooklyn, Watchtower Bible and Tract Society, 2005), 183–215.

22 *Organized to do Jehovah's will* (Brooklyn, NY, Watchtower Bible and Tract Society, 2005), 215.

23 "Parents—What Future Do You Want for Your Children?" *The Watchtower*, October 1, 2005, 30–31. http://wol.jw.org/en/wol/d/r1/lp-e/2005726. "Make Good Use of Changing Circumstances," *The Watchtower*, March 1, 2003, 22. http://wol.jw.org/en/wol/d/r1/lp-e/2003164.

24 *2014 Yearbook of Jehovah's Witnesses*. (Brooklyn: Watchtower Bible and Tract Society, 2013) 176. The calculation of two years does not take into account how many baptisms were of friends or children of Jehovah's witnesses so it may take even longer than

that to receive a single non-related convert.

25 "Do Jehovah's Witnesses Shun Former Members of Their Religion?" *jw.org* http://www.jw.org/en/jehovahs-witnesses/faq/shunning/.

26 "Is It Proper to Worship Jesus?" *Awake!*, April 8, 2000, 27. http://wol.jw.org/en/wol/d/r1/lp-e/102000250.

27 The subject of translating these previous passages has generated a vast amount of literature that can't be fully addressed in this answer. For a more in-depth treatment see Robert Bowman Jr., *Jehovah's Witnesses, Jesus Christ, and the Gospel of John* (Grand Rapids: Baker Books, 1989).

28 "What Jesus Taught About Himself" *The Watchtower*, April 1, 2010, 5. http://wol.jw.org/en/wol/d/r1/p-e/2010243.

29 See *Strong's Concordance* 2305 and 2320. As Peter T. O'Brien says in his commentary on Colossians: "*Theotes* ("deity") is the abstract noun from *theos* ("God") and is to be distinguished from *Theiotes* ("divine nature," "quality"), the abstract from *theios* ("divine," Rom 1:20; Wis. 18:19; cf. Lightfoot, 179, who illustrates the difference between the two nouns in Plutarch's *Moralia*). The former is *deitas*, the being God, i.e. the divine essence or Godhead; the latter is *divinitas*, i.e. the divine quality, godlikeness (Meyer, 358). Meyer adds: "Accordingly, the *essence* of God, undivided and in its whole fullness, dwells in Christ in his exalted state, so that He is the essential and adequate image of God (i. 15), which he could not be if he were not possessor of the divine 'essence.'" *Word Biblical Commentary: Vol. 44: Colossians, Philemon, 110.* See also W.E. Vine. *Vines Complete Expository Dictionary of Old and New Testament Words: With Topical Index* (Nashville, TN: Thomas Nelson, 1996) 178–179.

30 "The Lie That Made God a Mystery," *The Watchtower*, November 1, 2013, 5. http://wol.jw.org/en/wol/d/r1/lp-e/2013804.

31 "Why Follow 'the Christ'" *The Watchtower*, May 15, 2009, 29. http://wol.jw.org/en/wol/d/r1/lp-e/2009364.

32 *"Arche" Strong's Concordance*: 746, (a) rule (kingly or magisterial), (b) plural: in a quasi-personal sense, almost: rulers, magistrates, (c) beginning.

33 "What Jesus Taught About Himself," *The Watchtower*, April 1, 2010, 5. http://wol.jw.org/en/wol/d/r1/lp-e/2010243.

34 The technical terms for these cases are the "partitive genitive" and the "genitive of primacy."

35 "Who Is Michael the Archangel?" *Awake!*, February, 8 2002, 17. http://wol.jw.org/en/wol/d/r1/lp-e/102002085.

36 "Is Jesus the Archangel Michael?" *The Watchtower*, April 1, 2010, 19. http://wol.jw.org/en/wol/d/r1/lp-e/102002085.

37 Jason Evert. *Answering Jehovah's Witnesses* (El Cajon, CA: Catholic Answers, 2001), 74.

38 "Who Is Jesus Christ?" *The Watchtower*, September 15, 2005, 7. http://wol.jw.org/en/wol/d/r1/lp-e/2005681.

39 Oneness Pentecostals do deny that the Father and the Son are distinct persons. For a response see the Catholic Answers tract, "God in Three Persons" available online at www.catholic.com.

40 See *Catechism of the Catholic Church* paragraph 470.

41 "Jesus answered them, 'Destroy this temple, and in three days I will raise it up.' The Jews then said, 'It has taken forty-six years to build this temple, and will you raise it up in three days?" But he spoke of the temple of his body.'" (John 2:19–21).

42 *Should You Believe in the trinity? Is Jesus Christ the Almighty God?*

(Brooklyn: The Watchtower Bible and Tract Society, 1989), 7.

43 *Dialogue with Trypho*, 56,

44 *Exhortation to the Heathen,* 10.

45 *Against Praxeas,* 13.

46 Ibid, 5.

47 "The Lie That Made God A Mystery," *The Watchtower*, November, 1 2013, 5. http://www.jw.org/en/publications/magazines/wp20131101/lie-made-god-a-mystery-trinity/.

48 *Reasoning From the Scriptures* (Brooklyn: Watchtower Bible and Tract Society, 1989), 380–381.

49 Ibid. 381.

50 "The Lie That Made God A Mystery," *The Watchtower*, November, 1 2013, 5. http://www.jw.org/en/publications/magazines/wp20131101/lie-made-god-a-mystery-trinity/.

51 *Reasoning From the Scriptures* (Brooklyn: Watchtower Bible and Tract Society, 1989), 405.

52 "Is the Trinity a Bible teaching?" *The Watchtower*, March 1, 2012, 23. http://wol.jw.org/en/wol/d/r1/lp-e/2012173.

53 "The Lie That Made God A Mystery," *The Watchtower*, November, 1 2013, 5. http://www.jw.org/en/publications/magazines/wp20131101/lie-made-god-a-mystery-trinity/.

54 *Reasoning From the Scriptures* (Brooklyn: Watchtower Bible and Tract Society, 1989), 149.

55 *Against Praxeas,* 2.

56 According to the Jewish Encyclopedia, "Of the names of God in the Old Testament, that which occurs most frequently (6,823 times) is the so-called Tetragrammaton, YHWH, the distinctive personal name of the God of Israel. This name is commonly

represented in modern translations by the form "Jehovah,"
which, however, is a philological impossibility." "Names of God"
Jewish Encyclopedia (1906) http://www.jewishencyclopedia.com/
articles/11305-names-of-god.

57 "Does God Have a Name?" *The Watchtower*, February 1, 2009, 6.
http://wol.jw.org/en/wol/d/r1/lp-e/2009082.

58 "Why true Christians do not use the cross in worship" *jw.org*
http://www.jw.org/en/publications/books/bible-teach/why-true-
christians-do-not-use-the-cross-in-worship/.

59 Joseph Rutherford. *The Harp of God* (Brooklyn: Watchtower Bible
and Tract Society, 1921), 141.

60 Justin Martyr, *Dialogue with Trypho*, 40.

61 Tertullian, *Ad nationes*, 1.11.

62 Larry Hurtado, *The Earliest Christian Artifacts: Manuscripts and
Christian Origins* (Grand Rapids: Eerdmans, 2006), 135–54.

63 Walter Drum, "The Incarnation." *The Catholic Encyclopedia*. Vol.
7. (New York: Robert Appleton Company, 1910). http://www.
newadvent.org/cathen/07706b.htm Tertullian writes, "some among
you have dreamed that our god is an ass's head—an absurdity
which Cornelius Tacitus first suggested." *Ad nationes*, 1.11.

64 N.T. Wright, *The Resurrection of the Son of God* (Minneapolis:
Fortress Press, 2003), 469.

65 "A Closer Look at Some Myths About Death" *The Watchtower*,
June 1, 2002, 7–8. http://wol.jw.org/en/wol/d/r1/lp-e/2002401.

66 Ibid, 6.

67 For more see Tim Staples, "Seven proofs for the Immortality of
the Human Soul" *Catholic Answers Blog*, May 2, 2014, http://
www.catholic.com/blog/tim-staples/seven-proofs-for-the-

natural-immortality-of-the-human-soul.

68 "Myth 1: The Soul Is Immortal," *The Watchtower*, November 1, 2009, 4. http://wol.jw.org/en/wol/d/r1/lp-e/2009801.

69 "What Did Jesus Teach About Hell?" *The Watchtower*, November 1, 2008, 7–8. http://wol.jw.org/en/wol/d/r1/lp-e/2008802.

70 "Do All Faithful Christians Go to Heaven?" *The Watchtower*, June 1, 2011, 12. http://wol.jw.org/en/wol/d/r1/lp-e/2011405.

71 "Questions from Readers" *The Watchtower*, May 1, 2007, 31. http://wol.jw.org/en/wol/d/r1/lp-e/2007327.

72 Ibid.

73 *First Apology*, 66.

74 Pope John Paul II, *Redemptoris Missio*, 52.

75 *Awake!*, May 22, 1994, 2. "In former times thousands of youths died for putting God first. They are still doing it, only today the drama is played out in hospitals and courtrooms, with blood transfusions the issue."

76 In 1931 the Watchtower said, ""Vaccination is a direct violation of the everlasting covenant that God made with Noah after the flood." *Golden Age*, February 4, 1931, 293. But in 1952 the Watchtower said, "The matter of vaccination is one for the individual that has to face it to decide for himself." *The Watchtower*, December 15, 1952, 764.

77 "If a couple should decide to exclude the possibility of a pregnancy by using some form of contraception, that is their choice to make, and no one should judge them." "Is Contraception Morally Wrong?" *Awake!*, September 7, 2007, 11. http://wol.jw.org/en/wol/d/r1/lp-e/102007324.

78 Rochel Chein, "Is blood transfusions permissible in Jewish belief?"

chabad.org http://www.chabad.org/library/article_cdo/aid/625443/
jewish/Is-blood-transfusion-permissible-in-Jewish-belief.htm.

79 For more evidence for the primacy of Peter and the legitimacy
of apostolic succession see the Catholic Answers tracts available
online at www.catholic.com.

80 "Is the Pope 'Saint Peter's Successor?'" *The Watchtower*, August 1,
2011, 24. http://wol.jw.org/en/wol/d/r1/lp-e/2011571?q=peter&.

81 St. Augustine, "Against the Epistle of the Manicheans," in *Nicene and
Post-Nicene Fathers* (Grand Rapids, MI: Eerdman's, 1983) 4:130.

82 *Letter to the Corinthians*, 44:1–3.

83 *The Watchtower*, November 1, 1931, 327.

84 "Go On Walking as Jesus Christ Walked," *The Watchtower*,
September 15, 2005, 22. http://wol.jw.org/en/wol/d/r1/lp-
e/2005686?q=jesus+christ&p=par.

85 "Food at the Proper Time" *Annual Meeting Report*, 2012, http://
www.jw.org/en/jehovahs-witnesses/activities/events/annual-
meeting-report-2012/.

86 "Earnestly Seek Jehovah's Blessing" *The Watchtower*, September
15, 2010, 8–9. http://wol.jw.org/en/wol/d/r1/lp-e/2010682?q.

87 "They "'Keep Following the Lamb'" *The Watchtower*, September
15, 2009, 27. http://wol.jw.org/en/wol/d/r1/lp-e/2009123.

88 "Are You Prepared for Survival?" *The Watchtower*, May 15, 2006,
22. http://wol.jw.org/en/wol/d/r1/lp-e/2006366.

89 *The Watchtower*, March 1, 1981, 27.

90 *Organized to do Jehovah's will* (Brooklyn: Watchtower Bible and
Tract Society, 2005), 18.

91 Ibid. 19.

92 Increasing light from Jehovah continues to illuminate the path of his

people. It refines them organizationally, doctrinally, and morally." "Walking in the Path of Increasing Light," *The Watchtower*, February 15, 2006, 26. http://wol.jw.org/en/wol/d/r1/lp-e/2006126.

93 So, does Jehovah have a prophet to help them, to warn them of dangers and to declare things to come? These questions can be answered in the affirmative. Who is this prophet? . . . This "prophet" was not one man, but was a body of men and women. It was the small group of footstep followers of Jesus Christ, known at that time as International Bible Students. Today they are known as Jehovah's Christian witnesses." "'They shall know that a Prophet was among them," *The Watchtower*, April 1, 1972, 197–198.

94 "Do Not Be Quickly Shaken From Your Reason" *The Watchtower*, March 15, 1986, 14.

Become part of the team.
Help support Catholic Answers.

Catholic Answers is an apostolate dedicated to serving Christ by bringing the fullness of Catholic truth to the world. We help good Catholics become better Catholics, bring former Catholics "home," and lead non-Catholics into the fullness of the Faith.

Catholic Answers neither asks for nor receives financial support from any diocese. The majority of its annual income is in the form of donations from individual supporters like you.

To make a donation by phone using your credit card, please speak with one of our customer service representatives at 888-291-8000.

To make a donation by check, please send a check payable to "Catholic Answers" to:

> Catholic Answers
> 2020 Gillespie Way
> El Cajon, CA 92020

To make a donation online, visit **catholic.com**.

TO EXPLAIN & DEFEND THE FAITH

catholic.com